AF588065

Backwards, forwards across the sea

Yvonne Baker

Published by Cinnamon Press
www.cinnamonpress.com

The right of Yvonne Baker to be identified as author of this work has been asserted by her in accordance with the Copyright, Designs and Patent Act, 1988. © 2024, Yvonne Baker.
ISBN 978-1-78864-892-9

British Library Cataloguing in Publication Data. A CIP record for this book can be obtained from the British Library.

All rights reserved. No part of this publication may be reproduced, stored in a retrieval system, or transmitted in any form or by any means, electronic, mechanical, photocopying, recording or otherwise without the prior written permission of the publishers. This book may not be lent, hired out, resold or otherwise disposed of by way of trade in any form of binding or cover other than that in which it is published, without the prior consent of the publishers.

Designed and typeset in Bodini by Cinnamon Press. Cover design by Adam Craig © Adam Craig.

Cinnamon Press is represented by Inpress.

Acknowledgements

Thank you to the hard-working editors who accepted these poems, sometimes in earlier versions and with a different title.; *21 poems of childhood & education anthology* for the SCJ Competition — third prize: 'What if you could stand in that kitchen again' 2013; *The Frogmore papers:* 'Messages' *2015; The Emma Press Anthology of The Sea:* 'Distance' *2016;* Commended in the Second Light Poetry Competition: 'The Passport' 2019; ArtemisPOETRY: 'Joanna's House'

Grateful thanks are due to Mini Khalvati for her wisdom and advice on writing many of these poems, and I am particularly indebted to Myra Schneider for her encouragement, close reading and guidance over many years. Warmest thanks also to Jan Fortune for her encouragement to 'dig deeper', mentoring, and careful editing. My appreciation also to all at Cinnamon Press for the beautifully presented books and for accepting my work.

Contents

Door Field Light

Anastasia The door opens 13
The house in Greenside 14
Anastasia in the doorway 15
Shoes 16
Crossing 17
Returning home 18
My mother in the doorway 19
My grandmother's Christmas present to my mother 20
The field 21
Surviving 22
Kitchen doorway 23
My mother's story Leaving 24
The passport 25
The iron cooking pot 26
A walk in Cornwall 27
Messages 28
Legacy Elegy for my mother 29
Inheritance 30
Lintel 31
The mothers' race 32

My Irish Aunts and other saints

Seafarer 36
Encounter on a ferry with my great aunt Katy 37
Distance 38
Alone 39
Annie and St Pol 40
An upright woman 41
Out of breath 42
Shelly Winters' advice to Aunty Mary 44
What if you could stand in that kitchen again 45
Joanna's house 46
Shrine 47
The three Bridgets 48
Miracles 50
Translating the bones of St Cuthbert 51
My father's letters 52
Easter, 1916 53
The elephant aunts 54

For Tom, Caitlin, Jake, Beatrice and Miles,

with love

This is a thread of your story.

Backwards, forwards across the sea

Door Field Light

Anastasia

The door opens

Anastasia is always turning up these days.
She stands in a doorway that exists
on the borders of imagination, staring at a wall
someone has built between her house and the Green.

The doorway of my kitchen juts into the winter garden.
The apple tree is gnarled, canker eats its trunk.
There are no flowers, just dead leaves,
yet it's better than anything Anastasia knew.
Angled across the skyline, the tiled roofs seem
like half-open books that relinquish her story.
In fragments, my grandmother's life flutters down.

Now she steps quickly, bird-like, across the Green.
She is coming home from Oven Lane
after baking bread, hurrying through coarse grass
cattle hoofs have churned, swaddled in a shawl.

The house in Greenside

The book opens at Monet's house in Giverny,
but I'm elsewhere, walking towards

a patch of common land and a cottage,
where a woman leans on a half door.

Over the yellowed grass her daughters,
brandishing hurleys, trample the dry blades.

Her house is single-storey,
its white walls gleam in the late sun.

The shadow-play of trees makes me
forget the gloom inside, how wind

slips through the gaps, the damp
of stone, leaking roof.

The house is long gone, but I can build
a shelter for her story,

while she calls her daughters from the field
as if nothing else mattered.

Anastasia in the doorway

I've been looking at you for so long
through the lens of my mother's sadness.
Your feet are firmly earthed, your eyes
half closed as if the light is too harsh.

Maybe you're already suffering the headaches
that will swallow you in blackness, make
my mother grieve for you all her life,
and cause this image to haunt me.

Yet once I found a photo of your younger self
opening that door. Your hair loose, your face
lit with delight, it seemed as if you might run
across the threshold, into the bright day.

Shoes

Anastasia's grandparents owned a shop that sold
a fine array of boots and brogues. Its doorbell,

fragile as the clink of glass, summoned Grandfather Meany
from his room. Smiling, he'd retrieve from polished shelves

boxes of shoes with tiny buttons, sturdy lace-ups
brown and glossy as conkers.

But Anastasia's mother wed a labourer
so Anastasia never stepped inside the shop, nor the house

where her grandmother served tea from a silver pot.
She walked to church in cast-off shoes that pinched,

and knelt at the side, distant from the shopkeepers
in the centre isle — the unwritten rule for the poor.

Crossing

Newly married, she held
a cardboard suitcase full of hope
and faced the squalls of a winter sea.

But as Liverpool emerged dark
against the day's edge
the pull of home called her back
to a house that opened into a field
stretching the length of her life.

Returning there, she carried the rituals
of the past into a new century.

On the eve of St. Blaise, framed
in the door, she was still as a holy icon.
Surrounded by light, she held
strips of cloth to place later
on her children as a prayer.

In the last rays of the sun
she hung these remnants on a line
to invoke the saint's blessing.

St Blaise is the patron saint of sore throats.

Returning home

Her nervous hand shatters the small jug
she carried from home. A longing opens,
like a window filled with sky,
for the breath of cows in soft air, the dank
brown smell of the riverbank where crowfoot
and angelica grow and the heron waits for fish.

Yet when she goes back the light on the elm tree
has changed, the path to the house is not as remembered.
She must wait for another shift of the sun
for the peace she once knew to return.
Perhaps it happens as a warm smell of bread
fills the room, or, gathering sheets in
from the line, she glances upwards to see
swallows sweep the sky, settle in the eaves.

My mother in the doorway

i.m John

A small girl sits in the open door,
clutching a fold of Anastasia's skirt.

A blackbird's call spills under the low lintel.
Inside, a baby lies in a small box.

Eyes closed, his lashes cast blue shadows —
too still to be asleep.

The casket is carried from the house
through steady drizzle

and Anastasia, pulling her shawl tightly,
follows over the pocked grass.

The girl's sobbing echoes across the field,
where grey rain falls and falls.

My grandmother's Christmas present to my mother

When you slip into my wakefulness
at night, I try to understand
your part in my mother's story.

Tell me, do you remember that orange
you gave to your daughter,
realise what it meant to her?

It lit the winter room — delight
in its oily scent and pitted sheen
stayed with her all of her life.

But you are gone and cannot say.
Most likely, distracted by a boiling pot
or crying baby, you never noticed

a moment become fixed, in amber,
when a child gazed in wonder
at the small sun she rolled across the floor.

The field

Fair Green, Carrick-on-Suir

i)

The ancient field anchors the passing days.
At times Anastasia mistakes the ebb
and flow of the seasons
for contentment.
A breeze whispers the grass into waves.
The field, a windlass of green,
cranks memories from the deep —
a baby's tottering first step,
a small box carried to church in cold spring rain.
Some nights the field opens to the stars.
Tiny as speedwell,
these points of light are, like her family,
hurtling away from this place
faster than she can know.

ii)

Anastasia stands on the threshold,
watching a fox sniff in the shadows.
She turns towards the lit house,
the rock that her life
swirls and breaks against.
Across the field,
the shared earth-closet,
that must be cleaned tomorrow, sinks
into a sea of darkness.

Surviving

Her days never changed — cooking, cleaning,
a visit to church, gossiping with neighbours —

it was as though she lived under an unchanging sky.
Without washing machine or plastic bottle

she stepped lightly upon the earth
and had no need to fear choking the seas.

Yet newspapers warned of invasion, coal
and flour were scarce, and her children's letters

from London told of a fireplace suddenly exposed,
a dead man carried through a doorway on a chair.

A Christmas card — a prayer of hope for a daughter's
safety — still echoes her anxious love.

Kitchen doorway

Anastasia is standing at my kitchen door.
She's silent but I want answers.
And, since all I have are memories —
second-hand and thin as bees' wings —
this is the only way we can meet.

While she looks around my light-filled room
I long be in her kitchen with its glowing range,
a splinter of sun on a scrubbed table,
the fire burning with tales hidden in the coals.

Her life remains like a pool of darkened rainwater —
a sliver of sky, the underside of leaves.
And her secrets are safe in that kitchen,
its door opening to light,
a murmuring of bees.

My mother's story

Leaving

Carrick-on-Suir, 1938

Night. From a doorway
light falls
on furrows of darkened grass,
daisies white as surf.
A woman pauses,
as if to call a child —
a habit that wears away the heart.

Backwards, forwards across the sea.
And you, tossed between
the waves, liking England,
never quite settling,
your children losing the history
in the undertow.

The passport

London, 1943

Inside is your younger self,
a scarf around your head.
You've defaced this image,
scribbled a moustache and beard
across your mouth.

Holding it, I'm with you
under a cloud-dome of war.
You're perched on an armchair,
greasy with wear, while smoke
from your cigarette rises and curls.
Your missal, open on your lap,
is praying —
Salve me, fons pietatis —
but there's no comfort.

Between the *Bourjois* rouge
and *Craven A*, a telegram begs
Come home. Mammy is dying.
Your sisters have left for Ireland.
Your black dress and hat with its veil
still hang on the door.

You have implored the priest
in his cold house for help
but he doesn't know you
and won't sign your form.
Your missal will stay unopened
for years.
Gere curam mei finis.

Translations of the Latin extracts are from the Sequence in the Tridentine Mass for the Dead in my mother's missal:
Salve me, fons pietatis — Save me! O Save and comfort bring
Gere curam mei finis — Do not forsake me in the end

The iron cooking pot

London, 1949

You knew the tyranny
of the iron pot; a round-bellied god
it squatted on the range, its appetite
for coal and flames insatiable.

Water for washing, boiling the spuds —
your mother, face red, back aching,
never stopped until it was time to rake
the ash-filled altar, set the fire for morning.

You abandoned iron for aluminium.
Your stove with stubby legs turned on and off
but collected dust around its toes.
You bought bread, sliced from the Co-op —

yet as afternoons sighed into dusk,
you remembered your mother tracing a cross
on soda-dough, how a warm smell
from the black pot filled the room.

In a junk shop you found a pot painted
chalk-blue, but nothing could disguise
its dents. Planted with a red pelargonium
the colour became pallid, cold.

A walk in Cornwall

1950

You walk along the shore, lost
without your mother
and cradling the memory of a baby.
The world recedes.
The coastline stretches — grey beach and sea
under an aluminium sky.
Your footsteps disappear without trace
as you push against the wind,
clutch the neck of your coat.
You forget the dog following the waves,
the small child who trails behind.

Messages

Greenside, Carrick-on-Suir, 2002

The patch of grass with its ghost-houses
cried out to you all your life.
The last time you were in that field, a canary

free from its cage flew across your path.
And, like the early monks who thought seabirds
were departed souls, you knew the flutter
of yellow feathers was your mother saying goodbye.

Years later, gazing through the window,
you would be aware of your mother
by your shoulder and know that all was well.

But in that field with its ragged edge
of rosebay and cow parsley it was enough
that as shadows deepened in evening light
a bird flew out of the dusk, its wingbeat bright.

Legacy

Elegy for my mother

London, 2006

When you died the light shifted
and my world contracted like a field
at dusk, the edges frayed.

I sat in the garden and remembered
how you sent your love in a parcel.
The peony, you wrapped so carefully
for my birthday, fell apart.

Inheritance

London, 2008

Along with a tea-set and your love,
unwittingly you passed on the grief
you felt all your life at your mother's death.
Over and over, in a moth-grey dream
that haunted my childhood, you wouldn't wake.

The dream and tea-set stayed hidden until
peeling back tissue, creased, torn, I recalled
not sadness but times that made me smile.
The fuss with biscuits when clergy called,
the priest who preferred coffee and cake.

You loved the cup's impractical shape,
the fragile handle that was difficult to hold.
And generosity gleamed in its gold-edged gape
that lasted long after the tea grew cold.

Lintel

My grandmother sits in the light
of the open door turning the collar of a shirt.
Under a cloud-dome the day is mild,
the rhythm of her needle smooth.

Her daughters, who once ran in a field
on fire with the light of the declining sun
and shrieked through clouds of nettle spores,
are across the sea in England.

I want to tell her that her children will live
to old age, that her anxiety is ill founded.
But a glass wall of years separates us
and it's my reflection that haunts the scene.

On a day when the wind is lamming the clouds
her great great grandchildren are yelling
as they race across another field
to the swings beyond.

The mothers' race

A woman waiting for the iron to heat,
catches the sound of a Black and Tan's bullet,
the cry of a toddler outside the house.

Another returning to a room
where a small boy played, sees the space,
the window that opens to a wide sky.

The third reading a book, hears a bell,
opens the door to news
a child has fallen, his head bleeding.

Time judders   slowly slides forward   accelerates

as a woman, clasping a child, runs for help through still air
across the Green, hair flying free,
escaped from its pins

as a woman runs down the stairs in stockinged feet
into the calm afternoon, gasps for breath,
snatches the boy from the grass

as a woman runs through light like liquid honey
down the road towards the hospital,
leaving the front door open.

Breath caught in her chest,
each one races the length of her life,
running and running and running and running.

My Irish Aunts
and other saints

My Irish Aunts

showered their opinions
on an unsuspecting world.

Like Irish saints my aunts,
were never mealy-mouthed.

They didn't cure the sick
or raise the dead,

but if life rained misfortunes,
they would be there with an umbrella,

ready to remind you
that they told you to wear a raincoat.

Seafarer

for Ellen

Your sisters thought it was the WRNS
that unsettled you. But your war was spent
landlocked in a canteen, and the sea
was always part of Ireland's story.

Columbanus, full of firc, sct sail
in a curragh, light as the bones
of storm petrels, and you, demobbed,
braved the sea for New Zealand.

Cheerful letters of mince pies in summer
and the smiling photo with Santa, made
your sisters fear you would never return.
But you did, bringing me a Maori skirt.

But back home, trading travel
to be a housekeeper to a priest
was a life without meaning.
Was this why your mendicant life began?

A steadfast vision of a better future,
like those missionaries, who
climbed into fragile boats, squinted
at the horizon, found Ireland.

Encounter on a ferry with my great aunt Katy

My mother and her cousin, Cathleen,
scrabble in their bags. Cathleen whispers,
Pretend you haven't seen her.

But here she comes! Her crumpled skirt sways
in rhythm with the boat, narrowly
missing all in her way.

With a whiskey wheeze and without preamble,
she fumbles in the muddle
of her bag, lifts a clockwork toy.

Hands, paper-white and veined, tremble
as she winds it. *For my great-grandson,* she mumbles.
Two boxers, red painted shorts gleaming,

tiny arms in a synchronised judder,
punch and miss their mark until,
with a soft whirr, they shudder to a standstill.

Cathleen and my mother exchange a glance.
Well, my great aunt says,
I can't be talking to ye all day.

She lifts the toy into her bag, reverently,
and stumbles away, skirt rucked up behind her.
Aunty Katy, my mother calls anxiously.

But she's gone.
Making a holy show of herself! Cathleen sniffs
and snaps her bag shut.

Distance

for Barney

You are two years old when we bring you to this place —

where steps descend to a grey stone chapel, housing
the bones of a hermit

where waves grind against limestone cliffs
with low mutters

and where the water stretches to a distance so far
it makes you cry.

Years later, when you are living across the ocean,
I want to return there

to the rock that once grew around that holy man,
protecting him from harm

and where once you shouted at the sea — *It's too big.*

Alone

Skellig Michael, Co. Kerry

Enclosed in silence of moss and stone,
hours marked by plainchant, and days
bound by the Holy Rule, the monks
lived on a splinter of rock, facing
the white-wave distance.

One monk yearned to build his cell
closer to heaven, to be with the souls
of departed brothers — storm petrels
soaring in the vault of blue.
Clinging, to the rock-face he braved
spitting fulmars in his quest.

Yet peace was not found in an ascent
of bird into sky, but a plunge
into the deep waters of his heart.
Helpless against the winter tempest,
he was, at last, alone.

Annie and St Pol

for Nancy

On the rocky shore of Isle de Paz
St Pol expelled a lairdly worm
beneath the turbulent foam.

Bound tightly in a rust-red stole
the dragon struggled for a while
then sank into the deep.

Annie on an English shore
tried to banish melancholia
with brisk walks, cups of tea.

Yet each morning, among
dark sea-glass and kelp, her demons
wash up on ashen sands.

All the sea fetches in is gift.
But unlike the saints of early times,
Annie lacked the skills to overcome

wild beasts. Even so, she trailed
her sadness home, bravely —
made the best of it.

An upright woman

Those first days in Leamington Spa
Annie longed for Ireland and her squabbling sisters,

almost wished for the farmer with a turn in his eye
back in the half-asleep town.

When they moved to England, her sisters married.
Their noisy families in soft chairs, yelled

while the television roared. Annie, straight-backed
in the corner, refused a sherry at Christmas,

asked for weak tea in a thin-lipped cup.
Her sisters laughed, thought her odd.

Their families grew and changed direction.
Annie's path narrowed to her sometime home.

With sisters gone silence coated the rooms,
muffled the knock on the door.

Bubbling saucepans no longer disturbed the mornings,
afternoons drizzled to a standstill.

Days, when the wind keened, she worried the house
might lift in flight and, as her fears grew, she reached

for the bottle beside the cup with its pattern of faded roses.

Out of breath

for Stella

Stasia's the glamorous aunt, marrying
a man with a David Niven moustache,
racing along lanes on the back
of his motorbike.

Yet although her heart aches
for a house in a quiet road
and she begs him to sell the bike,
the love of speed never leaves her.

More Martha than Mary, she cleans
the stove in a breathless whirl,
makes cakes with a deft hand.
Her pace never slows.

Her home is a shrine for her dreams.
As a child she slept top to toe,
now the bed is mahogany,
the mattress is deep.

In the end, illness she sidestepped
for years slows her steps.
The table with the bowl, transparent
as a sigh, ceases to gleam.

When Stasia dies the house is still,
no longer breathing, despite
the endless chatter,
the rounds of sandwiches.

It's difficult to imagine her elsewhere
so I still think of her in the home
she loved, airing bedding
cajoling nieces to eat more.

Or, late afternoon, the bell rings,
and she realises it's Ellen,
her sister, arriving early
with several bags and a suitcase.

Shelly Winters' advice to Aunty Mary

Outside the Hendon Odeon we wait for the doors to open. You in a dogtooth coat, me in a school mac, trying to look older. Above us Shelly, leaning on a balcony, reveals her décolletage. We shuffle in the queue along the rain-black pavement.

The girl in the booth, barely lifts her lashes to check my age. Then we're munching toffees in the dark. I settle back — this'll be different from our visit to the ballet! But the film is unclear. Men in fancy dress prance, enter, exit. Distant gunfire echoes.

This is the year Kennedy is shot, Valentina Tereshkova circles the Earth with only the cold stars for company. My thoughts revolve around a boy, who doesn't notice me. Finally Shelly says we can go home, but that, too, won't be real.

So I go back to Latin homework and carrying a lacrosse stick on the bus. And soon you retire to Ireland to stand at the sink, stare at the night sky. News of gunfire in the North interrupts Radio Èireann's sentimental songs, while four Little Swans still dance across a stage and Shelly is only a bus ride away.

Shelley Winters starred as Irma in the film version of The Balcony *by Jean Genet in 1963.*

What if you could stand in that kitchen again

where the sun slanting through the window
stripes the blue table top,

the raspberry jelly, poured into waxed paper dishes,
forms a skin of light

and the remains of the cake mix, pale and gritty,
glistens in the bowl?

Suppose you scream you don't want a picnic,
hurl the bowl so it shatters

like the promise you would be home in time
for your brother's baptism.

But your aunt is smoothing her apron, pleased
to be giving you a treat;

the knife on the breadboard gleams,
the butter hard and shiny,

your voice scraped thin, falters.
And so, you eat the jelly-stained sandwiches

in a bus shelter that scoops up the weather,
listening to the gulls call harshly in the grey air.

The sea churns, wind scratches your face,
salt rain makes your eyes water,

you smile, say thank you, but the bread
swells in your throat.

Joanna's house

for Josie

The Child of Prague, a missing hand raised
in blessing, thrupenny-bit under his feet
for luck, jostled with *True Romance,*
hairnets, the brave smile in a tumbler.

She was the aunt who stayed.
Was this her choice? I never thought to ask.
A child-sized adult, a wild wind blew through her,
her house with its black range, never changed.

Cups and plates gleamed in a green press,
floral oilskin on a table caught the mid-day sun.
On a plate boiled bacon glistened, pale leaves
of cabbage shone with beads of fat.

Linoleum covered the floors —
its freezing slick made the stairs perilous
so when her foot missed a tread
she slipped from top to bottom.

Flat on her back, she lifted her eyes
to where Jesus, safe on the wall
smiled sadly, the light from his heart
radiating brightly, turning everything gold.

Shrine

for my great aunt, Mary

Pictures of saints — Patrick, Francis —
stared from the walls with shining faces.
The Virgin, garlanded with rosaries,
her open hands streamed with light.

As a child, the over-crowded bedroom,
its candles, plastic flowers
and my great aunt in her black shawl,
seemed part of a fairytale.

Later, a joke to be shared with friends.
I never thought the room might be
a comfort for loss of sisters, husband,
a much-loved son killed in war.

The three Bridgets

i)

Nothing could fetter Aunty Bridget.
Yet she kept a dog that only
snuffled the air when muzzled.
She loved it to distraction.

St. Brigid made a friend of a fox,
then gave him to the king.
Maybe she knew he'd escape,
that chains don't always tame.

ii)

When she wasn't turning bathwater
into beer for clergy, St Brigid prayed
her beauty might vanish.

Aunty Bridget in bright jumpers,
hair bleached, wore skirts just a little
too short, slipped from rooms lit
by a thread of winter light
into the brassy glare of a town pub.

She married a man
with an uncertain future in his blood.

iii)

My aunt once owned a fish and chip shop.

Confined to a backroom,
her husband, watched his limbs
dance to their own beat,
illness consume his life.
His days slid into shadows.

My aunt abandoned
the loud demands for cod
the heavy smell of fat,
for a man with a goat-beard
and slippery turn of phrase.
Her hair of faded gold
burning in the night rain.

Brigit, goddess of hearth and kitchen,
eventually became a saint.
In the convent, on the shrine
of the deity, nuns
still tend a sacred fire.

Miracles

Christina was herding sheep
when she fell. There was no one
to embrace her small body
or weep and stroke her hair;
but at her funeral she sat up,
floated to the ceiling, until
the priest called her back.
She thought it was her mother.

My aunt died at eight years old.
Her mother tucked her gently
into her small white box
and kissed her cold cheek.
But as the family gathered
to say the rosary, Hanorah
sat up and demanded
porridge for breakfast.

Christina Mirabilis lived around 1224.
A cult grew up around her.

Translating the bones of St Cuthbert

for Nigel

The monks of Lindisfarne bore
the remains over the causeway
to safety. Through jagged wind,
under a slate sky, they trudged
across Northumberland, praised
God even for the bitter rain.

Your ashes were carried
in a plastic green urn.
No hymns marked this crossing.
The dust of your turbulent life,
was poured into the earth
to where our parents lay.

Cuthbert was not left in peace
but moved from shrine to shrine,
amid a torrent of disputes.
This empty feeling doesn't matter,
I tell myself, at least you're
with those who loved you, at rest.

My father's letters

For over seventy years, they have lain
in their zipped leather cocoon. Creased,

and so thin the light almost shines through,
pages fluttering from the darkness of war.

Your voice is clear and open
in a way I can't remember in life.

I am longing and waiting to hear
from you darling, to know you are all right.

Sitting on the edge of a camp bed you wrote,
in careful loops and strokes,

about your anxieties, the tedium of the days,
your thoughts flying home.

I shall be glad to be home by the fire,
a good meal and to see your sweet face again.

You were as intent as the Lindisfarne scribe
perched on a stool in an Anglo-Saxon hut

in the half-light of winter, his hands cold
back aching, the vellum moist

with lapis and gold letters threatening to run,
as smoke from the fire faded in the damp air.

Easter, 1916

for my Irish grandfather

Tom fought with the British against the Boers.
Yet when the Great War loomed, older and weary
of combat, he battled instead to feed his family.

He hitched a lift in a farmer's cart past fields
of green barley, buckled under a downpour.
Head down, he tramped Waterford Docks for work.

Nights, between rows of bunks, talk hummed
around Ireland's growing unrest but Tom,
cold under a thin blanket, rolled into a black sleep.

Wednesday in Holy Week he returned home
in soft rain and, and sitting down by the roadside
among speedwell and bittercress, closed his eyes.

The shower stopped, a weak sun shone.
Although he might not see his house before dark
and unable to afford leather to mend his children's shoes,

that afternoon he was at peace, the sun
on his face and the scent of damp grass rising.

The elephant aunts

On the screen the orphans, wrapped
in blankets, with bottles of milk,
close their eyes; settle, trunks still.

Do they dream of their mother
in the wet-leaf smell of the forest,
and their aunts' protective love?

My aunts took me on holiday,
to the ballet, gave me a Maori skirt,
unwanted advice on my singing.

It's well known that when one elephant
dies, the others form a circle
to mourn it. Just so my aunts.

One by one, they took their place in the centre.

www.ingramcontent.com/pod-product-compliance
Ingram Content Group UK Ltd.
Pitfield, Milton Keynes, MK11 3LW, UK
UKHW040105210726
13892UKWH00005B/467